Wolves

Wolves

by Christina Wilsdon

Reader's Digest

Published by The Reader's Digest Association Limited
London • New York • Sydney • Montreal

CONTENTS

Chapter 1

Wolf pups grow up

A pack of grey wolves huddles together on a cold morning in early spring. Their warm breath makes clouds in the chilly air. But nearby one wolf is snug and warm in a den underground. Her furry body curls around five newborn pups. Each fuzzy brown pup is just 15 centimetres long – little more than the length of a £10 note.

The tiny pups squirm and whimper. They can't see, because their eyes are still tightly shut. They can't hear or walk yet, either. They can only creep by pulling themselves along with their front legs.

Scrabbling and shoving, the pups snuggle against their mother. Then they settle down as they drink her warm milk.

The mother wolf will live in the den with her pups for almost a month. She will step outside only to pass waste and to drink water. Her mate and the other wolves in the pack will hunt and bring her food.

Growing pups

A wolf pup weighs about half a kilo when born. It gains a kilo or so a week during the first 14 weeks of its life. Its baby blue eyes turn yellow by the time it is four months old.

Two weeks go by. The pups open their eyes, which are blue. They can walk now, and their baby teeth are growing. When they are three weeks old, the pups leave the den for the first time. The rest of the pack greets them eagerly. They sniff the pups from nose to tail. The pups jump at the big wolves, pawing them and licking their faces.

The whole pack helps to care for the pups. They guard them as they play outside the den. A grown-up wolf even baby-sits if the mother goes hunting with the pack.

All the wolves help to feed the pups, too, carrying food to them in their stomachs. When the pups lick and nuzzle the adult's mouth, the wolf coughs up food for them.

By the time the pups are nine weeks old, they stop drinking milk and eat only meat. They look more like adult wolves now, but their heads and feet are still too big for their bodies. Their coats are a mixture of puppy fuzz and adult hair.

DID YOU KNOW?

Wolf pups lose their baby teeth, just like human children do. Their permanent teeth have grown by the time the pups are six months old and ready to hunt with the pack.

The pups' world is limited to the area outside their den for their first weeks of life. But they find lots to do. The chubby little wolves chase mice and chew sticks. They wrestle and romp. They climb onto adult wolves that are trying to nap and bite their tails!

When the pups are a little older, their world grows a bit bigger. They travel with the pack to a new place called a rendezvous site. Now the pups can explore an even bigger area. For the next few weeks, this site will be where all the pack will meet. Then they will all move to a different rendezvous site.

By the time the pups are six months old, they are nearly as big as adult wolves. They are strong enough to learn the hunting skills they need to survive.

Their first winter is harsh and cold, but there are plenty of deer for food. The pups eat well and grow stronger. In spring, the year-old pups are fully grown at last and help to bring food to their mother as she raises a new litter in the old den.

To stay or go it alone?

A wolf has a decision to make when it grows up. It can stay with the pack and help to raise its younger brothers and sisters. Or it can leave when it is about two years old and find a mate. A wolf that leaves the pack also leaves the pack's territory. It strikes out to find a new home of its own.

Chapter 2

The body of a wolf

A wolf's paw can be up to 14 centimetres long. Tough pads and long claws help the wolf to climb rocks and grip the ground when it runs.

DID YOU KNOW?

A wolf can leap nearly 5 metres in a single bound – almost half the length of a double-decker bus!

Wild dogs

What furry animal wags its tail, loves to play and howls? You would be right if you guessed either 'wolf' or 'dog'. The wolf is the ancestor of all dogs. Some dogs, such as huskies, look a lot like wolves. Other dogs, like poodles, don't.

Grey wolves are the biggest wild dogs. A large male wolf can be nearly 2 metres long from nose to tail. If you put a ruler next to his shoulder, he will stand almost a metre tall.

Much of this height comes from a wolf's legs. Long legs are good for running.

Scientists have recorded wolves sprinting at speeds up to 30 miles per hour – as fast as a car goes in towns or villages.

A wolf can run at top speed only for a little while. But it can trot for many hours at 5 miles per hour – the speed of a person walking briskly. It can also lope at 20 miles per hour for about 20 minutes while chasing prey. That's as fast as a good 100 metre sprinter.

Why does a wolf need to be a good runner? Because it eats deer, moose and caribou – animals that run even faster.

Wolf senses

A wolf uses its sharp senses to find food. Its sense of smell is especially keen. Wolves can smell other animals from a distance of about 300 metres – nearly the length of three football pitches. One scientist watched a pack of wolves catch the scent of moose that were 1½ miles away. That's a length of nearly 24 football pitches!

A wolf also has excellent hearing. It can hear a wolf that is howling several miles away. Each ear can swivel in different directions to locate the source of a sound.

A wolf's eyes are good at spotting movement and seeing in low light. This helps the wolf to hunt at dawn, dusk and at night. But a wolf's eyes are not able to pick out details.

The eyes of a wolf are positioned toward the front of its head, like ours. This helps the wolf to judge distances. A deer, on the other hand, has its eyes on the sides of its head. This helps it to see nearly all around without even moving its head. Eyes like these help the deer to watch out for danger – such as a hungry wolf stalking it.

My, what big teeth you have...

Wolves are carnivores – meat eaters. Like all carnivores, adult wolves have strong, sharp teeth. They can cut through a thick rope with one single bite! An adult wolf has 42 teeth. Four teeth are sharp fangs for holding onto prey.

Wolves need to have
sensitive ears and
noses to help them
to find food, because
their eyesight is not
very sharp.

Pups in the same litter
sometimes grow adult coats
that are different colours.

Coat of many colours

Grey wolves are not always grey. They can be white, creamy or black. Their coats can also be shades of brown, tan and red. Even a grey wolf's 'grey' fur is made up of different shades of grey sprinkled with white, brown and black hairs.

Wolves that live in the far north tend to be lighter in colour than wolves farther south. Most of the wolves that live on the snowy arctic tundra in Canada are white. Those living in Alaska, however, tend to be grey. Wolves in the forests farther south are usually grey or black.

A wolf gets its colour from the long, stiff hairs in its coat called 'guard hairs'. These hairs grow 12-13 centimetres long on its shoulders and back. They work like a raincoat to shed water. Closer to the wolf's skin is a layer of short, fluffy fur that keeps it warm.

Grey wolf pups are born with fuzzy brown or grey coats. They change into their adult colours when they begin to grow guard hairs.

Chapter 3

Wolf packs

People may tell scary stories
about huge wolf packs, with
hundreds of animals. In reality,
wolf packs have fewer than
20 wolves and usually consist
of only four to eight wolves.

Life in the wild

A wolf can live alone. It can catch small animals, such as mice, rabbits and beavers. And it can even kill a deer or moose by itself. But a wolf's life is easier and safer if it is part of a pack.

The pack is the wolf's family. It is usually made up of two parents and their young of different ages. Some packs may also include aunts, uncles, cousins or other wolves that are not related.

All the wolves in a pack work together to catch food and take care of the pups. They defend their home, or territory, from other wolves. A pack's territory is where it roams, hunts and raises its young.

Top dogs

The leader of the pack is a strong male wolf. He is often called the alpha male. His mate is known as the alpha female. These two alpha wolves are the only pair in the pack that mate and have pups.

The other wolves in the pack obey the alphas. But these other wolves are not equals. Each wolf has its own place in the pack above or below the other wolves. This place is called a rank.

A wolf can only boss around, or dominate, a wolf of lower rank. A ranking system like this is called a dominance order.

Family life

A dominance order helps wolves to get along with one another. Each wolf knows its place, so it is not always squabbling with other wolves to get its way. Instead, the wolves can work together to survive.

Still, wolves in a pack sometimes quarrel. If you watch a pack of wolves, you may see bared teeth and hear snarls and growls. But you will also see wagging tails and friendly licks. This behaviour is all part of how wolves communicate.

Wolves use body language to be friendly, too. A grown-up wolf may greet its father by acting like a puppy begging for food. Maybe you have even seen a dog greet a person in this way.

Wolves also 'talk' with their tails. A dominant wolf holds its tail high in the air. A low-ranking wolf holds its tail down. Wolves also wag their tails when they're being friendly, just as dogs do.

Wolves 'talk' to each other
with their faces and bodies.
An angry wolf may bare its
teeth, wrinkle its forehead
and point its ears forward.

27

Baby's first howl

A wolf pup can howl when it is just two weeks old.

A wolf that is by itself may use a special 'lonesome howl' to call its pack.

Owoooo!

Wolves use sounds to communicate. They whimper and squeak to be friendly and growl when angry. They may bark if excited or alarmed. But wolves are most famous for howling.

A wolf's howl is a low, mournful cry. It rises and falls like a long, slow song. Other wolves often join in. Scientists have found that humans can hear a wolf's howl from 4 miles away. A wolf can probably hear a howl from an even greater distance.

Wolves howl for many reasons. Howling brings the pack together. It helps pack members to keep in touch when they are separated. Howling may also remind other packs to stay out of the wolves' territory.

No trespassing!

Have you ever taken a dog for a walk and stopped at almost every tree? Pet dogs use urine to mark territory with their scent to communicate with other dogs. Wolves do this, too. This behaviour is called scent marking. A wolf may also rub its body on objects and scratch the ground to leave its scent.

Wolves mark trees, rocks and other objects in their territory. These scent marks mean 'No trespassing'! If a strange wolf wanders into the territory, a few sniffs will warn it to leave. Scent marking may be a way of 'building fences' between the territories of different packs.

Chapter 4

Hungry as a wolf

Teamwork

Wolves in a pack work as a team to hunt large animals, such as moose, deer, elk, wild sheep and bison. Arctic wolves also hunt caribou and musk-oxen.

Wolves find prey as they travel across their territory. Sometimes the wolves smell prey before they see it. Then they follow their noses and sneak up on the animals. Other times wolves may see a herd from a hilltop or surprise a sleeping animal.

When wolves get close to their prey, they creep towards it. The prey may not notice the danger until the wolves suddenly rush at it.

Once in a while, however, the prey refuses to run away. A big, strong moose, for example, may simply stand and stare at the wolves until they give up.

Usually, wolves attack animals that are young, old, sick or injured. These are the easiest animals to catch because they are the weakest and cannot keep up with the herd when the wolves are chasing them. But wolves are also strong and fast enough to catch healthy animals.

wild WORDS

prey   animals that are
        hunted by other
        animals for food.

A pack of wolves on the chase looks
ferocious, but the wolves will give up
after running a few miles. They may also
give up if an animal fights back. Then the
wolves go off to find easier prey.

A wolf's world

Deer, moose and other prey are not the only animals in the wolf's world. Wolves also share their habitat with animals that are not prey – including other predators.

In some places, these predators are bears. Most of the time, bears and wolves have nothing to do with one another. But if a bear stumbles across a wolf pack's prey, the wolves usually run away. Then the bear gets a free meal.

Mountain lions and coyotes – American wolf-like prairie dogs – have a more difficult time with wolves. Scientists recently discovered that wolves in Montana, USA chase mountain lions away from their meals. Wolves don't like coyotes and will chase and even kill them.

DID YOU KNOW?

Ravens seem to have a special bond with wolves. They follow wolves when they see them hunting. The big black birds even fly above wolf trails, looking for wolves. Wolves sometimes seem to play with ravens. The birds tease the wolves into leaping at them, then fly away at the very last second. Then the ravens start the game again!

Hungry wolves don't hunt only big prey, such as deer. Wolves often eat beavers and hares. They can even survive on mice.

Chapter 5

Wolves
in the world

Scientists and others try to persuade people that these wild dogs are not the 'big bad wolves' of fairy tales.

Where wolves live

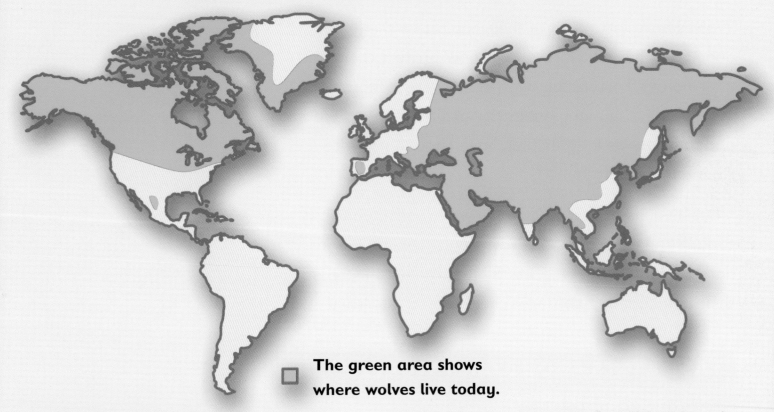

□ **The green area shows where wolves live today.**

Just 200 years ago, many kinds of grey wolves roamed the world from the Arctic to the Mediterranean. In America, their territory extended from the far north down to Mexico.

But, for decades, wolves were hunted and killed and worldwide their numbers have rapidly diminished and some species have become extinct. There are now no grey wolves in the southern USA although there are still large numbers – as many as 60,000 – in Alaska and Canada.

In the UK wolves have become extinct. But, elsewhere in Europe, where they are now a protected species, there are thought to be up to 18,000 grey wolves. And thousands of wolves still live in the wilds of northern Russia.

The future of wolves

Wolves have lost much of their habitat as the human population has grown, but laws now protect them and their homes. Fortunately, wolves are very adaptable. They can live in many habitats – prairies, forests, woods and tundra – as long as they have enough room to roam and prey to hunt.

But humans are still the wolf's worst enemy and organisations such as the World Wildlife Fund work hard to change the way we think of them, to increase their numbers and conserve their natural territory.

FAST FACTS ABOUT GREY WOLVES

SCIENTIFIC NAME	*Canis lupus*
CLASS	Mammals
ORDER	*Carnivora*
SIZE	Up to 1 metre tall at the shoulder
WEIGHT	Males to 80 kilos Females to 50 kilos
LIFESPAN	About 10 years in the wild About 13 years in captivity
HABITAT	Forests, woods, tundra and plains
TOP SPEED	About 30 miles per hour

GLOSSARY OF *Wild* WORDS

alpha wolf	a wolf that is a leader in its pack
ancestor	an animal from whom others are descended
caribou	reindeer
carnivore	an animal that eats meat
dominance order	a system in which some wolves in a pack have a higher rank than other wolves

ferocious	fierce, savage
genus	closely related species
habitat	the natural environment where an animal or plant lives
litter	a group of pups born at the same time
pack	a family or group of wolves that live together

predator	an animal that hunts and eats other animals to survive	species	a category of living things that are closely related to one another
prey	animals that are hunted for food by other animals	sprinting	running as fast as possible for a short distance
rendezvous site	an area used by a pack of wolves with young pups	territory	an area defended by a wolf pack
roam	to wander	tundra	cold, snowy northern lands that lack forests

INDEX

CREDITS

Front Cover: Brand X Pictures; 1 Dynamic Graphics, Inc.; 3 Getty Images Ltd/Digital Vision;
4-5 Corel Professional Photos; 6-7 Getty Images Ltd/PhotoDisc; 8 Image 100;
9 Dynamic Graphics, Inc.; 10-15 Dynamic Graphics, Inc.; 16 Corbis;
18-19 Corel Professional Photos; 20-23 Getty Images Ltd/PhotoDisc;
24 Dynamic Graphics, Inc.; 25 Corel Professional Photos; 26-27 Dynamic Graphics, Inc.;
28 Getty Images Ltd/Digital Vision; 28 L Corel Professional Photos; 30-31 Image 100;
32-34 Getty Images Ltd/Digital Vision; 36-37 Dynamic Graphics, Inc.;
38-39 Getty Images Ltd/PhotoDisc; 40 Dynamic Graphics, Inc.;
42-43 Corel Professional Photos; 44-45 Dynamic Graphics, Inc.;
47 Getty Images Ltd/PhotoDisc; 48 Dynamic Graphics, Inc.;
Back Cover: Dynamic Graphics, Inc.

Wolves is an *All About Animals* fact book
published by The Reader's Digest Association, Inc.

Written by Christina Wilsdon

Copyright © 2005 The Reader's Digest Association, Inc.
This edition was adapted and published in 2008 by
The Reader's Digest Association Limited
11 Westferry Circus, Canary Wharf, London E14 4HE
Reprinted in 2010

Editor: Rachel Warren Chadd
Designer: Nicola Liddiard
Art editor: Simon Webb

We are committed both to the quality of our products and the service we provide
to our customers. We value your comments, so please do contact us on
08705 113366 or via our website at www.readersdigest.co.uk

If you have any comments or suggestions about the content of our books,
email us at gbeditorial@readersdigest.co.uk

Printed in China

Reader's
Digest

ISBN: 978 0 276 44323 7
Book code: 640-006 UP0000-2
Oracle code: 504500064H.00.24